D1621024

# Teachings of Jesus

**NELSON/REGENCY**

*Nashville*

**Teachings of Jesus**
Copyright © 1992 by Thomas Nelson, Inc.

3 4 5 6 7 8 9 10 — 96 95 94 93 92

🎋 🎋 🎋 🎋 🎋 🎋 🎋 🎋 🎋 🎋 🎋 🎋 🎋 🎋 🎋

# Contents

❄ ❄ ❄ ❄ ❄ ❄ ❄ ❄ ❄ ❄ ❄ ❄ ❄ ❄

# The Sermon on the Mount

*And Jesus, when He came out, saw the great multitude and was moved with compassion for them, because they were like sheep not having a shepherd. So He began to teach them many things.*

—Mark 6:34

❊ ❊ ❊ ❊ ❊ ❊ ❊ ❊ ❊ ❊ ❊ ❊ ❊ ❊ ❊

# MATTHEW 5

### 1

*And seeing the multitudes, He went up on a mountain, and when He was seated His disciples came to Him.*

### 2

*Then He opened His mouth and taught them, saying:*

### 3

*"Blessed are the poor in spirit,*

*For theirs is the kingdom of*
*heaven.*

4

*Blessed are those who mourn,*
*For they shall be comforted.*

5

*Blessed are the meek,*
*For they shall inherit the*
*earth.*

6

*Blessed are those who hunger*

� � � � � � � � �

and thirst for
righteousness,
For they shall be filled.

7

Blessed are the merciful,
For they shall obtain mercy.

8

Blessed are the pure in heart,
For they shall see God.

9

Blessed are the peacemakers,

❋ ❋ ❋ ❋ ❋ ❋ ❋ ❋ ❋ ❋ ❋ ❋ ❋ ❋ ❋ ❋

*For they shall be called sons
of God.*

## 10

*Blessed are those who are
persecuted for
righteousness' sake,
For theirs is the kingdom of
heaven.*

## 11

*"Blessed are you when they revile
and persecute you, and say all kinds*

❧ ❧ ❧ ❧ ❧ ❧ ❧ ❧ ❧ ❧ ❧ ❧ ❧ ❧ ❧

of evil against you falsely for My sake.

## 12

"Rejoice and be exceedingly glad, for great is your reward in heaven, for so they persecuted the prophets who were before you.

## 13

"You are the salt of the earth; but if the salt loses its flavor, how shall it be seasoned? It is then good for noth-

ing but to be thrown out and tram-
pled underfoot by men.

## 14

"You are the light of the world. A
city that is set on a hill cannot be
hidden.

## 15

"Nor do they light a lamp and put it
under a basket, but on a lampstand,
and it gives light to all who are in
the house.

## 16

"Let your light so shine before men, that they may see your good works and glorify your Father in heaven.

## 17

"Do not think that I came to destroy the Law or the Prophets. I did not come to destroy but to fulfill.

## 18

"For assuredly, I say to you, till heaven and earth pass away, one jot

❀ ❀ ❀ ❀ ❀ ❀ ❀ ❀ ❀ ❀ ❀ ❀ ❀ ❀ ❀

or one tittle will by no means pass from the law till all is fulfilled.

### 19

"Whoever therefore breaks one of the least of these commandments, and teaches men so, shall be called least in the kingdom of heaven; but whoever does and teaches them, he shall be called great in the kingdom of heaven.

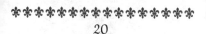

## 20

"For I say to you, that unless your righteousness exceeds the righteousness of the scribes and Pharisees, you will by no means enter the kingdom of heaven.

## 21

"You have heard that it was said to those of old, 'You shall not murder, and whoever murders will be in danger of the judgment.'

❀ ❀ ❀ ❀ ❀ ❀ ❀ ❀ ❀ ❀ ❀ ❀ ❀ ❀

## 22

"But I say to you that whoever is angry with his brother without a cause shall be in danger of the judgment. And whoever says to his brother, 'Raca!' shall be in danger of the council. But whoever says, 'You fool!' shall be in danger of hell fire.

## 23

"Therefore if you bring your gift to the altar, and there remember that

❀ ❀ ❀ ❀ ❀ ❀ ❀ ❀ ❀ ❀ ❀ ❀ ❀ ❀ ❀ ❀

*your brother has something against you,*

### 24

"*leave your gift there before the altar, and go your way. First be reconciled to your brother, and then come and offer your gift.*

### 25

"*Agree with your adversary quickly, while you are on the way with him, lest your adversary deliver you to the*

❊ ❊ ❊ ❊ ❊ ❊ ❊ ❊ ❊ ❊ ❊ ❊ ❊ ❊ ❊

judge, the judge hand you over to the officer, and you be thrown into prison.

### 26

"Assuredly, I say to you, you will by no means get out of there till you have paid the last penny.

### 27

"You have heard that it was said to those of old, 'You shall not commit adultery.'

❀ ❀ ❀ ❀ ❀ ❀ ❀ ❀ ❀ ❀ ❀ ❀ ❀ ❀ ❀ ❀

## 28

"But I say to you that whoever looks at a woman to lust for her has already committed adultery with her in his heart.

## 29

"If your right eye causes you to sin, pluck it out and cast it from you; for it is more profitable for you that one of your members perish, than for your whole body to be cast into hell.

❈ ❈ ❈ ❈ ❈ ❈ ❈ ❈ ❈ ❈ ❈ ❈ ❈ ❈ ❈ ❈

### 30

*"And if your right hand causes you to sin, cut it off and cast it from you; for it is more profitable for you that one of your members perish, than for your whole body to be cast into hell.*

### 31

*"Furthermore it has been said, 'Whoever divorces his wife, let him give her a certificate of divorce.'*

❀ ❀ ❀ ❀ ❀ ❀ ❀ ❀ ❀ ❀ ❀ ❀ ❀ ❀ ❀

## 32

"But I say to you that whoever divorces his wife for any reason except sexual immorality causes her to commit adultery; and whoever marries a woman who is divorced commits adultery.

## 33

"Again you have heard that it was said to those of old, 'You shall not *swear falsely, but shall perform your oaths to the Lord.'*

34

*"But I say to you, do not swear at all: neither by heaven, for it is God's throne;*

35

*"nor by the earth, for it is His footstool; nor by Jerusalem, for it is the city of the great King.*

## 36

"Nor shall you swear by your head, because you cannot make one hair white or black.

## 37

"But let your 'Yes' be 'Yes,' and your 'No,' 'No.' For whatever is more than these is from the evil one.

## 38

"You have heard that it was said,

'An eye for an eye and a tooth for a tooth.'

## 39

"But I tell you not to resist an evil person. But whoever slaps you on your right cheek, turn the other to him also.

## 40

"If anyone wants to sue you and take away your tunic, let him have your cloak also.

### 41

*"And whoever compels you to go one mile, go with him two.*

### 42

*"Give to him who asks you, and from him who wants to borrow from you do not turn away.*

### 43

*"You have heard that it was said, 'You shall love your neighbor and hate your enemy.'*

❀ ❀ ❀ ❀ ❀ ❀ ❀ ❀ ❀ ❀ ❀ ❀ ❀ ❀

## 44

*"But I say to you, love your enemies, bless those who curse you, do good to those who hate you, and pray for those who spitefully use you and persecute you,*

## 45

*"that you may be sons of your Father in heaven; for He makes His sun rise on the evil and on the good, and sends rain on the just and on the unjust.*

## 46

*"For if you love those who love you, what reward have you? Do not even the tax collectors do the same?*

## 47

*"And if you greet your brethren only, what do you do more than others? Do not even the tax collectors do so?*

## 48

*"Therefore you shall be perfect, just as your Father in heaven is perfect.*

❀ ❀ ❀ ❀ ❀ ❀ ❀ ❀ ❀ ❀ ❀ ❀ ❀ ❀

# MATTHEW 6

## 1

*"Take heed that you do not do your charitable deeds before men, to be seen by them. Otherwise you have no reward from your Father in heaven.*

## 2

*"Therefore, when you do a charitable deed, do not sound a trumpet before you as the hypocrites do in the*

✿ ✿ ✿ ✿ ✿ ✿ ✿ ✿ ✿ ✿ ✿ ✿ ✿ ✿

synagogues and in the streets, that they may have glory from men. Assuredly, I say to you, they have their reward.

### 3

"But when you do a charitable deed, do not let your left hand know what your right hand is doing,

### 4

"that your charitable deed may be in secret; and your Father who sees

in secret will Himself reward you
openly.

## 5

"And when you pray, you shall not
be like the hypocrites. For they love to
pray standing in the synagogues and
on the corners of the streets, that they
may be seen by men. Assuredly, I say
to you, they have their reward.

## 6

"But you, when you pray, go into

❀ ❀ ❀ ❀ ❀ ❀ ❀ ❀ ❀ ❀ ❀ ❀ ❀ ❀ ❀

your room, and when you have shut your door, pray to your Father who is in the secret place; and your Father who sees in secret will reward you openly.

### 7

"And when you pray, do not use vain repetitions as the heathen do. For they think that they will be heard for their many words.

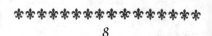

## 8

*"Therefore do not be like them. For your Father knows the things you have need of before you ask Him.*

## 9

*"In this manner, therefore, pray:*

> *Our Father in heaven,*
> *Hallowed be Your name.*

## 10

*Your kingdom come.*

✾✾✾✾✾✾✾✾✾✾✾✾✾✾✾✾

*Your will be done*
*On earth as it is in heaven.*

### 11

*Give us this day our daily*
*bread.*

### 12

*And forgive us our debts,*
*As we forgive our debtors.*

### 13

*And do not lead us into*
*temptation,*

❀❀❀❀❀❀❀❀❀❀❀❀❀❀❀❀

*But deliver us from the evil one.*
*For Yours is the kingdom and*
*the power and the glory*
*forever. Amen.*

### 14

"*For if you forgive men their tres-*
*passes, your heavenly Father will also*
*forgive you.*

### 15

"*But if you do not forgive men their*

✿ ✿ ✿ ✿ ✿ ✿ ✿ ✿ ✿ ✿ ✿ ✿ ✿ ✿ ✿

trespasses, neither will your Father forgive your trespasses.

### 16

"Moreover, when you fast, do not be like the hypocrites, with a sad countenance. For they disfigure their faces that they may appear to men to be fasting. Assuredly, I say to you, they have their reward.

### 17

"But you, when you fast, anoint your head and wash your face,

❀ ❀ ❀ ❀ ❀ ❀ ❀ ❀ ❀ ❀ ❀ ❀ ❀ ❀

## 18

*"so that you do not appear to men to be fasting, but to your Father who is in the secret place; and your Father who sees in secret will reward you openly.*

## 19

*"Do not lay up for yourselves treasures on earth, where moth and rust destroy and where thieves break in and steal;*

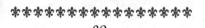

## 20

"but lay up for yourselves treasures in heaven, where neither moth nor rust destroys and where thieves do not break in and steal.

## 21

"For where your treasure is, there your heart will be also.

## 22

"The lamp of the body is the eye. If

✿ ✿ ✿ ✿ ✿ ✿ ✿ ✿ ✿ ✿ ✿ ✿ ✿ ✿ ✿

therefore your eye is good, your whole body will be full of light.

### 23

"But if your eye is bad, your whole body will be full of darkness. If therefore the light that is in you is darkness, how great is that darkness!

### 24

"No one can serve two masters; for either he will hate the one and love the other, or else he will be loyal to

❁ ❁ ❁ ❁ ❁ ❁ ❁ ❁ ❁ ❁ ❁ ❁ ❁ ❁

the one and despise the other. You
cannot serve God and mammon.

### 25

"Therefore I say to you, do not
worry about your life, what you will
eat or what you will drink; nor
about your body, what you will put
on. Is not life more than food and
the body more than clothing?

### 26

"Look at the birds of the air, for they

neither sow nor reap nor gather into barns; yet your heavenly Father feeds them. Are you not of more value than they?

### 27

"Which of you by worrying can add one cubit to his stature?

### 28

"So why do you worry about clothing? Consider the lilies of the field,

*how they grow: they neither toil nor spin;*

## 29

*"and yet I say to you that even Solomon in all his glory was not arrayed like one of these.*

## 30

*"Now if God so clothes the grass of the field, which today is, and tomorrow is thrown into the oven, will He*

not much more clothe you, O you of little faith?

## 31

"Therefore do not worry, saying, 'What shall we eat?' or 'What shall we drink?' or 'What shall we wear?'

## 32

"For after all these things the Gentiles seek. For your heavenly Father knows that you need all these things.

### 33

"But seek first the kingdom of God and His righteousness, and all these things shall be added to you.

### 34

"Therefore do not worry about tomorrow, for tomorrow will worry about its own things. Sufficient for the day is its own trouble.

❧ ❧ ❧ ❧ ❧ ❧ ❧ ❧ ❧ ❧ ❧ ❧ ❧ ❧

# MATTHEW 7

## 1

*"Judge not, that you be not judged.*

## 2

*"For with what judgment you judge, you will be judged; and with the measure you use, it will be measured back to you.*

## 3

*"And why do you look at the speck*

in your brother's eye, but do not consider the plank in your own eye?

### 4

"Or how can you say to your brother, 'Let me remove the speck from your eye'; and look, a plank is in your own eye?

### 5

"Hypocrite! First remove the plank from your own eye, and then you

❀ ❀ ❀ ❀ ❀ ❀ ❀ ❀ ❀ ❀ ❀ ❀ ❀ ❀ ❀ ❀

will see clearly to remove the speck from your brother's eye.

### 6

"Do not give what is holy to the dogs; nor cast your pearls before swine, lest they trample them under their feet, and turn and tear you in pieces.

### 7

"Ask, and it will be given to you;

❀ ❀ ❀ ❀ ❀ ❀ ❀ ❀ ❀ ❀ ❀ ❀ ❀ ❀ ❀

seek, and you will find; knock, and it
will be opened to you.

8

"For everyone who asks receives, and
he who seeks finds, and to him who
knocks it will be opened.

9

"Or what man is there among you
who, if his son asks for bread, will
give him a stone?

❀ ❀ ❀ ❀ ❀ ❀ ❀ ❀ ❀ ❀ ❀

## 10

"Or if he asks for a fish, will he give him a serpent?

## 11

"If you then, being evil, know how to give good gifts to your children, how much more will your Father who is in heaven give good things to those who ask Him!

## 12

"Therefore, whatever you want men

❋ ❋ ❋ ❋ ❋ ❋ ❋ ❋ ❋ ❋ ❋ ❋ ❋ ❋ ❋ ❋

to do to you, do also to them, for this is the Law and the Prophets.

### 13

"Enter by the narrow gate; for wide is the gate and broad is the way that leads to destruction, and there are many who go in by it.

### 14

"Because narrow is the gate and difficult is the way which leads to life, and there are few who find it.

❀ ❀ ❀ ❀ ❀ ❀ ❀ ❀ ❀ ❀ ❀ ❀ ❀ ❀ ❀

### 15

"Beware of false prophets, who come to you in sheep's clothing, but inwardly they are ravenous wolves.

### 16

"You will know them by their fruits. Do men gather grapes from thornbushes or figs from thistles?

### 17

"Even so, every good tree bears good fruit, but a bad tree bears bad fruit.

❄ ❄ ❄ ❄ ❄ ❄ ❄ ❄ ❄ ❄ ❄ ❄ ❄ ❄

### 18

*"A good tree cannot bear bad fruit, nor can a bad tree bear good fruit.*

### 19

*"Every tree that does not bear good fruit is cut down and thrown into the fire.*

### 20

*"Therefore by their fruits you will know them.*

## 21

"Not everyone who says to Me, 'Lord, Lord,' shall enter the kingdom of heaven, but he who does the will of My Father in heaven.

## 22

"Many will say to Me in that day, 'Lord, Lord, have we not prophesied in Your name, cast out demons in Your name, and done many wonders in Your name?'

❀ ❀ ❀ ❀ ❀ ❀ ❀ ❀ ❀ ❀ ❀ ❀ ❀ ❀

### 23

"And then I will declare to them, 'I never knew you; depart from Me, you who practice lawlessness!'

### 24

"Therefore whoever hears these sayings of Mine, and does them, I will liken him to a wise man who built his house on the rock:

### 25

"and the rain descended, the floods

came, and the winds blew and beat on that house; and it did not fall, for it was founded on the rock.

### 26

"But everyone who hears these sayings of Mine, and does not do them, will be like a foolish man who built his house on the sand:

### 27

"and the rain descended, the floods

❀ ❀ ❀ ❀ ❀ ❀ ❀ ❀ ❀ ❀ ❀ ❀ ❀ ❀ ❀ ❀

came, and the winds blew and beat on that house; and it fell. And great was its fall.''

### 28

And so it was, when Jesus had ended these sayings, that the people were astonished at His teaching,

### 29

for He taught them as one having authority, and not as the scribes.

# The Parables of Jesus

"I will open My mouth in parables;
I will utter things kept secret from the
foundation of the world."

—Matthew 13:35

# THE PARABLE OF THE SOWER

## Mark 4

1
*And again He began to teach by the sea. And a great multitude was gathered to Him, so that He got into a boat and sat in it on the sea; and the whole multitude was on the land facing the sea.*

❀ ❀ ❀ ❀ ❀ ❀ ❀ ❀ ❀ ❀ ❀ ❀ ❀ ❀ ❀

### 2

*Then He taught them many things by parables, and said to them in His teaching:*

### 3

*"Listen! Behold, a sower went out to sow.*

### 4

*"And it happened, as he sowed, that some seed fell by the wayside; and the birds of the air came and devoured it.*

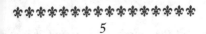

### 5

"Some fell on stony ground, where it did not have much earth; and immediately it sprang up because it had no depth of earth.

### 6

"But when the sun was up it was scorched, and because it had no root it withered away.

### 7

"And some seed fell among thorns;

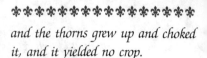

and the thorns grew up and choked it, and it yielded no crop.

### 8

"But other seed fell on good ground and yielded a crop that sprang up, increased and produced: some thirtyfold, some sixty, and some a hundred."

### 9

And He said to them, "He who has ears to hear, let him hear!"

## 10

*But when He was alone, those around Him with the twelve asked Him about the parable.*

## 11

*And He said to them, "To you it has been given to know the mystery of the kingdom of God; but to those who are outside, all things come in parables,*

❀ ❀ ❀ ❀ ❀ ❀ ❀ ❀ ❀ ❀ ❀ ❀ ❀ ❀

## 12

"so that

    *'Seeing they may see and not*
        *perceive,*
    *And hearing they may hear*
        *and not understand;*
    *Lest they should turn,*
    *And their sins be forgiven*
        *them.'*"

### 13

And He said to them, "Do you not understand this parable? How then will you understand all the parables?

### 14

"The sower sows the word.

### 15

"And these are the ones by the wayside where the word is sown. When they hear, Satan comes immediately

❖ ❖ ❖ ❖ ❖ ❖ ❖ ❖ ❖ ❖ ❖ ❖ ❖ ❖ ❖

and takes away the word that was sown in their hearts.

## 16

"These likewise are the ones sown on stony ground who, when they hear the word, immediately receive it with gladness;

## 17

"and they have no root in themselves, and so endure only for a time.

Afterward, when tribulation or per-
secution arises for the word's sake,
immediately they stumble.

### 18

"Now these are the ones sown
among thorns; they are the ones who
hear the word,

### 19

"and the cares of this world, the de-
ceitfulness of riches, and the desires

for other things entering in choke the word, and it becomes unfruitful.

### 20

"But these are the ones sown on good ground, those who hear the word, accept it, and bear fruit: some thirty-fold, some sixty, and some a hundred."

❧❧❧❧❧❧❧❧❧❧❧❧❧❧❧

# THE PARABLE OF THE
# WHEAT AND THE TARES
## Matthew 13

### 24

*Another parable He put forth to them, saying: "The kingdom of heaven is like a man who sowed good seed in his field;*

### 25

*"but while men slept, his enemy*

❧ ❧ ❧ ❧ ❧ ❧ ❧ ❧ ❧ ❧ ❧ ❧ ❧ ❧ ❧

came and sowed tares among the
wheat and went his way.

### 26

"But when the grain had sprouted
and produced a crop, then the tares
also appeared.

### 27

"So the servants of the owner came
and said to him, 'Sir, did you not
sow good seed in your field? How
then does it have tares?'

28

*"He said to them, 'An enemy has done this.' The servants said to him, 'Do you want us then to go and gather them up?'*

29

*"But he said, 'No, lest while you gather up the tares you also uproot the wheat with them.*

30

*'Let both grow together until the*

harvest, and at the time of harvest I will say to the reapers, "First gather together the tares and bind them in bundles to burn them, but gather the wheat into my barn."''"

❦ ❦ ❦ ❦ ❦ ❦ ❦ ❦ ❦ ❦ ❦ ❦ ❦ ❦ ❦

# THE PARABLE OF THE MUSTARD SEED
## Matthew 13

### 31

*Another parable He put forth to them, saying: "The kingdom of heaven is like a mustard seed, which a man took and sowed in his field,*

### 32

*"which indeed is the least of all the seeds; but when it is grown it is*

❀ ❀ ❀ ❀ ❀ ❀ ❀ ❀ ❀ ❀ ❀ ❀ ❀ ❀ ❀ ❀

*greater than the herbs and becomes a
tree, so that the birds of the air come
and nest in its branches."*

# THE PARABLE OF THE LEAVEN
## Matthew 13

33
*Another parable He spoke to them: "The kingdom of heaven is like leaven, which a woman took and hid in three measures of meal till it was all leavened."*

❀ ❀ ❀ ❀ ❀ ❀ ❀ ❀ ❀ ❀ ❀ ❀ ❀ ❀ ❀

# THE PARABLE OF THE
# HIDDEN TREASURE
## Matthew 13

### 44

*"Again, the kingdom of heaven is like treasure hidden in a field, which a man found and hid; and for joy over it he goes and sells all that he has and buys that field."*

❧ ❧ ❧ ❧ ❧ ❧ ❧ ❧ ❧ ❧ ❧ ❧ ❧ ❧ ❧

# THE PARABLE OF THE PEARL OF GREAT PRICE
## Matthew 13

### 45

*"Again, the kingdom of heaven is like a merchant seeking beautiful pearls,*

### 46

*"who, when he had found one pearl of great price, went and sold all that he had and bought it."*

❀ ❀ ❀ ❀ ❀ ❀ ❀ ❀ ❀ ❀ ❀ ❀ ❀ ❀

# THE PARABLE OF THE
# GOOD SAMARITAN
## Luke 10

### 25

*And behold, a certain lawyer stood up and tested Him, saying, "Teacher, what shall I do to inherit eternal life?"*

### 26

*He said to him, "What is written in the law? What is your reading of it?"*

*So he answered and said, " 'You shall love the LORD your God with all your heart, with all your soul, with all your strength, and with all your mind,' and 'your neighbor as yourself.' "*

28

*And He said to him, "You have answered rightly; do this and you will live."*

❧ ❧ ❧ ❧ ❧ ❧ ❧ ❧ ❧ ❧ ❧ ❧ ❧ ❧

### 29

*But he, wanting to justify himself, said to Jesus, "And who is my neighbor?"*

### 30

*Then Jesus answered and said: "A certain man went down from Jerusalem to Jericho, and fell among thieves, who stripped him of his clothing, wounded him, and departed, leaving him half dead.*

❀ ❀ ❀ ❀ ❀ ❀ ❀ ❀ ❀ ❀ ❀ ❀ ❀ ❀ ❀

## 31

*"Now by chance a certain priest came down that road. And when he saw him, he passed by on the other side.*

## 32

*"Likewise a Levite, when he arrived at the place, came and looked, and passed by on the other side.*

## 33

*"But a certain Samaritan, as he*

❀ ❀ ❀ ❀ ❀ ❀ ❀ ❀ ❀ ❀ ❀ ❀ ❀ ❀ ❀

journeyed, came where he was. And when he saw him, he had compassion.

## 34

"So he went to him and bandaged his wounds, pouring on oil and wine; and he set him on his own animal, brought him to an inn, and took care of him.

## 35

"On the next day, when he departed,

he took out two denarii, gave them to the innkeeper, and said to him, 'Take care of him; and whatever more you spend, when I come again, I will repay you.'

36
"So which of these three do you think was neighbor to him who fell among the thieves?"

### 37

*And he said, "He who showed mercy on him." Then Jesus said to him, "Go and do likewise."*

❀ ❀ ❀ ❀ ❀ ❀ ❀ ❀ ❀ ❀ ❀ ❀ ❀ ❀

# THE PARABLE OF
# THE LOST SHEEP
## Matthew 18

### 10

*"Take heed that you do not despise one of these little ones, for I say to you that in heaven their angels always see the face of My Father who is in heaven.*

❄ ❄ ❄ ❄ ❄ ❄ ❄ ❄ ❄ ❄ ❄ ❄ ❄ ❄ ❄

## 11

"For the Son of Man has come to save that which was lost.

## 12

"What do you think? If a man has a hundred sheep, and one of them goes astray, does he not leave the ninety-nine and go to the mountains to seek the one that is straying?

❀ ❀ ❀ ❀ ❀ ❀ ❀ ❀ ❀ ❀ ❀ ❀ ❀ ❀

### 13

"And if he should find it, assuredly, I say to you, he rejoices more over that sheep than over the ninety-nine that did not go astray.

### 14

"Even so it is not the will of your Father who is in heaven that one of these little ones should perish."

## THE PARABLE OF THE UNFORGIVING SERVANT
### Matthew 18

21

*Then Peter came to Him and said, "Lord, how often shall my brother sin against me, and I forgive him? Up to seven times?"*

22

*Jesus said to him, "I do not say to*

you, up to seven times, but up to seventy times seven.

23
"Therefore the kingdom of heaven is like a certain king who wanted to settle accounts with his servants.

24
"And when he had begun to settle accounts, one was brought to him who owed him ten thousand talents.

## 25

"But as he was not able to pay, his master commanded that he be sold, with his wife and children and all that he had, and that payment be made.

## 26

"The servant therefore fell down before him, saying, 'Master, have patience with me, and I will pay you all.'

## 27

"Then the master of that servant was moved with compassion, released him, and forgave him the debt.

## 28

"But that servant went out and found one of his fellow servants who owed him a hundred denarii; and he laid hands on him and took him by the throat, saying, 'Pay me what you owe!'

❧ ❧ ❧ ❧ ❧ ❧ ❧ ❧ ❧ ❧ ❧ ❧ ❧ ❧

## 29

*"So his fellow servant fell down at his feet and begged him, saying, 'Have patience with me, and I will pay you all.'*

## 30

*"And he would not, but went and threw him into prison till he should pay the debt.*

## 31

*"So when his fellow servants saw*

what had been done, they were very grieved, and came and told their master all that had been done.

## 32

"Then his master, after he had called him, said to him, 'You wicked servant! I forgave you all that debt because you begged me.

## 33

'Should you not also have had com-

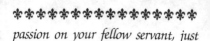

*passion on your fellow servant, just as I had pity on you?'*

### 34

"And his master was angry, and delivered him to the torturers until he should pay all that was due to him.

### 35

"So My heavenly Father also will do to you if each of you, from his heart, does not forgive his brother his trespasses."

# THE PARABLE OF THE GREAT SUPPER
## Luke 14

**15**

*Now when one of those who sat at the table with Him heard these things, he said to Him, "Blessed is he who shall eat bread in the kingdom of God!"*

**16**

*Then He said to him, "A certain*

❋ ❋ ❋ ❋ ❋ ❋ ❋ ❋ ❋ ❋ ❋ ❋ ❋ ❋ ❋

man gave a great supper and invited many,

## 17

"and sent his servant at supper time to say to those who were invited, 'Come, for all things are now ready.'

## 18

"But they all with one accord began to make excuses. The first said to him, 'I have bought a piece of

ground, and I must go and see it. I ask you to have me excused.'

## 19

"And another said, 'I have bought five yoke of oxen, and I am going to test them. I ask you to have me excused.'

## 20

"Still another said, 'I have married a wife, and therefore I cannot come.'

❀ ❀ ❀ ❀ ❀ ❀ ❀ ❀ ❀ ❀ ❀ ❀ ❀ ❀ ❀

## 21

"So that servant came and reported these things to his master. Then the master of the house, being angry, said to his servant, 'Go out quickly into the streets and lanes of the city, and bring in here the poor and the maimed and the lame and the blind.'

## 22

"And the servant said, 'Master, it is done as you commanded, and still there is room.'

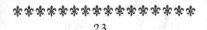

### 23

"Then the master said to the servant, 'Go out into the highways and hedges, and compel them to come in, that my house may be filled.

### 24

'For I say to you that none of those men who were invited shall taste my supper.' "

## THE PARABLE OF THE GROWING SEED
### Mark 4

26

*And He said, "The kingdom of God is as if a man should scatter seed on the ground,*

27

*"and should sleep by night and rise by day, and the seed should sprout*

❧ ❧ ❧ ❧ ❧ ❧ ❧ ❧ ❧ ❧ ❧ ❧ ❧ ❧ ❧ ❧

and grow, he himself does not know
how.

### 28

"For the earth yields crops by itself:
first the blade, then the head, after
that the full grain in the head.

### 29

"But when the grain ripens, immediately he puts in the sickle, because
the harvest has come."

✤ ✤ ✤ ✤ ✤ ✤ ✤ ✤ ✤ ✤ ✤ ✤ ✤ ✤ ✤

# THE PARABLE OF THE WISE AND FOOLISH VIRGINS
## Matthew 25

### 1

*"Then the kingdom of heaven shall be likened to ten virgins who took their lamps and went out to meet the bridegroom.*

✣ ✣ ✣ ✣ ✣ ✣ ✣ ✣ ✣ ✣ ✣ ✣ ✣ ✣ ✣

### 2

*"Now five of them were wise, and five were foolish.*

### 3

*"Those who were foolish took their lamps and took no oil with them,*

### 4

*"but the wise took oil in their vessels with their lamps.*

### 5

"But while the bridegroom was delayed, they all slumbered and slept.

### 6

"And at midnight a cry was heard: 'Behold, the bridegroom is coming; go out to meet him!'

### 7

"Then all those virgins arose and trimmed their lamps.

## 8

"And the foolish said to the wise, 'Give us some of your oil, for our lamps are going out.'

"But the wise answered, saying, 'No, lest there should not be enough for us and you; but go rather to those who sell, and buy for yourselves.'

❊ ❊ ❊ ❊ ❊ ❊ ❊ ❊ ❊ ❊ ❊ ❊ ❊ ❊ ❊

## 10

"And while they went to buy, the bridegroom came, and those who were ready went in with him to the wedding; and the door was shut.

## 11

"Afterward the other virgins came also, saying, 'Lord, Lord, open to us!'

## 12

"But he answered and said, 'As-

*surely, I say to you, I do not know you.'*

### 13

*"Watch therefore, for you know neither the day nor the hour in which the Son of Man is coming."*

## THE PARABLE OF THE TALENTS
### Matthew 25

14

*"For the kingdom of heaven is like a man traveling to a far country, who called his own servants and delivered his goods to them.*

15

*"And to one he gave five talents, to another two, and to another one, to*

*each according to his own ability; and immediately he went on a journey.*

### 16

*"Then he who had received the five talents went and traded with them, and made another five talents.*

### 17

*"And likewise he who had received two gained two more also.*

❊ ❊ ❊ ❊ ❊ ❊ ❊ ❊ ❊ ❊ ❊ ❊ ❊ ❊ ❊ ❊

## 18

"But he who had received one went and dug in the ground, and hid his lord's money.

## 19

"After a long time the lord of those servants came and settled accounts with them.

## 20

"So he who had received five talents came and brought five other talents,

saying, 'Lord, you delivered to me five talents; look, I have gained five more talents besides them.'

### 21

"His lord said to him, 'Well done, good and faithful servant; you were faithful over a few things, I will make you ruler over many things. Enter into the joy of your lord.'

### 22

"He also who had received two talents came and said, 'Lord, you delivered to me two talents; look, I have gained two more talents besides them.'

23

"His lord said to him, 'Well done, good and faithful servant; you have been faithful over a few things, I will make you ruler over many things. Enter into the joy of your lord.'

### 24

"Then he who had received the one talent came and said, 'Lord, I knew you to be a hard man, reaping where you have not sown, and gathering where you have not scattered seed.

### 25

'And I was afraid, and went and hid your talent in the ground. Look, there you have what is yours.'

❁ ❁ ❁ ❁ ❁ ❁ ❁ ❁ ❁ ❁ ❁ ❁ ❁ ❁

## 26

"But his lord answered and said to him, 'You wicked and lazy servant, you knew that I reap where I have not sown, and gather where I have not scattered seed.

## 27

'So you ought to have deposited my money with the bankers, and at my coming I would have received back my own with interest.

## 28

'Therefore take the talent from him, and give it to him who has ten talents.

## 29

'For to everyone who has, more will be given, and he will have abundance; but from him who does not have, even what he has will be taken away.

❁ ❁ ❁ ❁ ❁ ❁ ❁ ❁ ❁ ❁ ❁ ❁ ❁ ❁
## 30
'And cast the unprofitable servant into the outer darkness. There will be weeping and gnashing of teeth.' "

✿ ✿ ✿ ✿ ✿ ✿ ✿ ✿ ✿ ✿ ✿ ✿ ✿ ✿ ✿

# THE PARABLE OF THE ABSENT HOUSEHOLDER
## Mark 13

### 32

*"But of that day and hour no one knows, not even the angels in heaven, nor the Son, but only the Father.*

### 33

*"Take heed, watch and pray; for you do not know when the time is.*

34

*"It is like a man going to a far country, who left his house and gave authority to his servants, and to each his work, and commanded the doorkeeper to watch.*

35

*"Watch therefore, for you do not know when the master of the house is coming—in the evening, at midnight, at the crowing of the rooster, or in the morning—*

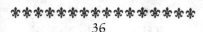

### 36

"lest, coming suddenly, he find you sleeping.

### 37

"And what I say to you, I say to all: Watch!"

❋ ❋ ❋ ❋ ❋ ❋ ❋ ❋ ❋ ❋ ❋ ❋ ❋ ❋

# THE PARABLE OF
# THE PHARISEE AND
# THE TAX COLLECTOR
## Luke 18

### 9

*Also He spoke this parable to some who trusted in themselves that they were righteous, and despised others:*

### 10

*"Two men went up to the temple to*

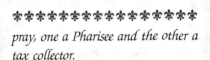

pray, one a Pharisee and the other a tax collector.

## 11

"The Pharisee stood and prayed thus with himself, 'God, I thank You that I am not like other men—extortioners, unjust, adulterers, or even as this tax collector.

## 12

'I fast twice a week; I give tithes of all that I possess.'

❀ ❀ ❀ ❀ ❀ ❀ ❀ ❀ ❀ ❀ ❀ ❀ ❀ ❀

## 13

"And the tax collector, standing afar off, would not so much as raise his eyes to heaven, but beat his breast, saying, 'God, be merciful to me a sinner!'

## 14

"I tell you, this man went down to his house justified rather than the other; for everyone who exalts himself will be humbled, and he who humbles himself will be exalted."

## THE PARABLE OF THE UNPROFITABLE SERVANT
### Luke 17

7

*"And which of you, having a servant plowing or tending sheep, will say to him when he has come in from the field, 'Come at once and sit down to eat'?*

8

*"But will he not rather say to him,*

'Prepare something for my supper, and gird yourself and serve me till I have eaten and drunk, and afterward you will eat and drink'?

### 9

"Does he thank that servant because he did the things that were commanded him? I think not.

### 10

"So likewise you, when you have done all those things which you are

❀ ❀ ❀ ❀ ❀ ❀ ❀ ❀ ❀ ❀ ❀ ❀ ❀ ❀ ❀

*commanded, say, 'We are unprofit-able servants. We have done what was our duty to do.' "*